by Iain Gray

Lang**Syne**

PUBLISHING

WRITING *to* REMEMBER

LangSyne

PUBLISHING

WRITING *to* REMEMBER

79 Main Street, Newtongrange,
Midlothian EH22 4NA
Tel: 0131 344 0414   Fax: 0845 075 6085
E-mail: info@lang-syne.co.uk
www.langsyneshop.co.uk

Design by Dorothy Meikle
Printed by Printwell Ltd
© Lang Syne Publishers Ltd 2016

ISBN 978-1-85217-528-3

Lloyd

MOTTO:
Without God without anything,
God is enough.

CREST:
A silver wolf supporting
a spear's head in its paws.

NAME variations include:
Lloid
Llwyd
Loyd
Lwyd

Chapter one:

The origins of popular surnames

by George Forbes and Iain Gray

If you don't know where you came from, you won't know where you're going is a frequently quoted observation and one that has a particular resonance today when there has been a marked upsurge in interest in genealogy, with increasing numbers of people curious to trace their family roots.

Main sources for genealogical research include census returns and official records of births, marriages and deaths – and the key to unlocking the detail they contain is obviously a family surname, one that has been 'inherited' and passed from generation to generation.

No matter our station in life, we all have a surname – but it was not until about the middle of the fourteenth century that the practice of being identified by a particular surname became commonly established throughout the British Isles.

Previous to this, it was normal for a person to be identified through the use of only a forename.

But as population gradually increased and there were many more people with the same forename, surnames were adopted to distinguish one person, or community, from another.

Many common English surnames are patronymic in origin, meaning they stem from the forename of one's father – with 'Johnson,' for example, indicating 'son of John.'

It was the Normans, in the wake of their eleventh century conquest of Anglo-Saxon England, a pivotal moment in the nation's history, who first brought surnames into usage – although it was a gradual process.

For the Normans, these were names initially based on the title of their estates, local villages and chateaux in France to distinguish and identify these landholdings.

Such grand descriptions also helped enhance the prestige of these warlords and generally glorify their lofty positions high above the humble serfs slaving away below in the pecking order who had only single names, often with Biblical connotations as in Pierre and Jacques.

The only descriptive distinctions among the peasantry concerned their occupations, like 'Pierre the swineherd' or 'Jacques the ferryman.'

Roots of surnames that came into usage in England not only included Norman-French, but also Old French, Old Norse, Old English, Middle English, German, Latin, Greek, Hebrew and the Gaelic languages of the Celts.

The Normans themselves were originally Vikings, or 'Northmen', who raided, colonised and eventually settled down around the French coastline.

The had sailed up the Seine in their longboats in 900AD under their ferocious leader Rollo and ruled the roost in north eastern France before sailing over to conquer England in 1066 under Duke William of Normandy – better known to posterity as William the Conqueror, or King William I of England.

Granted lands in the newly-conquered England, some of their descendants later acquired territories in Wales, Scotland and Ireland – taking not only their own surnames, but also the practice of adopting a surname, with them.

But it was in England where Norman rule and custom first impacted, particularly in relation to the adoption of surnames.

This is reflected in the famous *Domesday Book*, a massive survey of much of England and Wales, ordered by William I, to determine who owned what, what it was worth and therefore how much they were liable to pay in taxes to the voracious Royal Exchequer.

Completed in 1086 and now held in the National Archives in Kew, London, 'Domesday' was an Old English word meaning 'Day of Judgement.'

This was because, in the words of one contemporary chronicler, "its decisions, like those of the Last Judgement, are unalterable."

It had been a requirement of all those English landholders – from the richest to the poorest – that they identify themselves for the purposes of the survey and for future reference by means of a surname.

This is why the *Domesday Book*, although written in Latin as was the practice for several centuries with both civic and ecclesiastical records, is an invaluable source for the early appearance of a wide range of English surnames.

Several of these names were coined in connection with occupations.

These include Baker and Smith, while Cooks, Chamberlains, Constables and Porters were to be found carrying out duties in large medieval households.

The church's influence can be found in names such as Bishop, Friar and Monk while the popular name of Bennett derives from the late fifth to mid-sixth century Saint Benedict, founder of the Benedictine order of monks.

The carly medical profession is represented by Barber, while businessmen produced names that include Merchant and Sellers.

Down at the village watermill, the names that cropped up included Millar/Miller, Walker and Fuller, while other self-explanatory trades included Cooper, Tailor, Mason and Wright.

Even the scenery was utilised as in Moor, Hill, Wood and Forrest – while the hunt and the chase supplied names that include Hunter, Falconer, Fowler and Fox.

Colours are also a source of popular surnames, as in Black, Brown, Gray/Grey, Green and White, and would have denoted the colour of the clothing the person habitually wore or, apart from the obvious exception of 'Green', one's hair colouring or even complexion.

The surname Red developed into Reid, while

Blue was rare and no-one wanted to be associated
with yellow.

Rather self-important individuals took surnames
that include Goodman and Wiseman, while physical
attributes crept into surnames such as Small and Little.

Many families proudly boast the heraldic
device known as a Coat of Arms, as featured on our
front cover.

The central motif of the Coat of Arms would
originally have been what was borne on the shield of
a warrior to distinguish himself from others on the
battlefield.

Not featured on the Coat of Arms, but high-
lighted on page three, is the family motto and related
crest – with the latter frequently different from the
central motif.

Adding further variety to the rich cultural
heritage that is represented by surnames is the
appearance in recent times in lists of the 100 most
common names found in England of ones that include
Khan, Patel and Singh – names that have proud roots
in the vast sub-continent of India.

Echoes of a far distant past can still be found
in our surnames and they can be borne with pride in
commemoration of our forebears.

Chapter two:

Ancient Britons

Although a popular surname throughout England today, 'Lloyd' is nevertheless particularly identified with Wales.

It stems from the personal name 'Lloyd' or 'Llwd', derived in turn from 'clywd' or 'ilwyd' indicating 'grey' or 'brown' and was perhaps originally descriptive of someone of grey or brown hair colouring or who habitually wore clothing of either of these colours.

The lives and times of bearers of the name, however, were much more colourful than the original meaning of the name may indicate.

Although, in common with many other surnames, 'Lloyd' as a surname was popularised in the wake of the Norman Conquest of 1066, the ancestors of some of those who would later adopt it pre-date the arrival on British shores of invaders such as the Romans, Vikings, Anglo-Saxons and Normans.

This means that flowing through the veins of many bearers of the Lloyd name today is the blood of the ancient Britons.

Of Celtic pedigree, these early inhabitants of the British Isles were settled for centuries from a line south of the River Forth in Scotland all the way down to the south coast of England and with a particular presence in Wales.

Speaking a Celtic language known as Brythonic, they boasted a glorious culture that flourished even after the Roman invasion of Britain in 43 AD and the subsequent consolidation of Roman power by about 84 AD.

With many of the original Britons absorbing aspects of Roman culture, they became 'Romano-British' – while still retaining their own proud Celtic heritage.

Following the withdrawal of the last Roman legions from Britain in 406, what is now modern-day Wales, or *Cymru*, fragmented into a number of independent kingdoms – with the most powerful king being regarded as overall ruler.

Recognised as King of the Britons, he had to battle with not only internal rivals but also the depredations of the wild sea rovers known as the Vikings, or Northmen.

There were also the Anglo-Saxons to contend with – as those Germanic tribes who invaded and settled in the south and east of the island of Britain from about the early fifth century were known.

They were composed of the Jutes, from the area of the Jutland Peninsula in modern Denmark, the Saxons from Lower Saxony, in modern Germany and the Angles from the Angeln area of Germany, and it was the Angles who gave the name 'Engla land', or 'Aengla land' – better known as 'England.'

The Anglo-Saxons held sway in what became England from approximately 550 to 1066, with the main kingdoms those of Sussex, Wessex, Northumbria, Mercia, Kent, East Anglia and Essex.

Whoever controlled the most powerful of these kingdoms was tacitly recognised as overall 'king' – one of the most noted being Alfred the Great, King of Wessex from 871 to 899.

The Anglo-Saxons, meanwhile, had usurped the power of the indigenous Britons, such as those found in Wales, and who referred to them as 'Saeson' or 'Saxones.'

It is from this that the Scottish Gaelic term for 'English people' of 'Sasannach' derives, the Irish Gaelic 'Sasanach' and the Welsh 'Saeson.'

The death knell of Anglo-Saxon supremacy and also what remained of Welsh independence was sounded with the Norman Conquest and the defeat of Harold II at the battle of Hastings.

By 1066, England had become a nation with several powerful competitors to the throne.

In what were extremely complex family, political and military machinations, the king was Harold II, who had succeeded to the throne following the death of Edward the Confessor.

But his right to the throne was contested by two powerful competitors – his brother-in-law King Harold Hardrada of Norway, in alliance with Tostig, Harold II's brother, and Duke William II of Normandy.

In what has become known as The Year of Three Battles, Hardrada invaded England and gained victory over the English king on September 20 at the battle of Fulford, in Yorkshire.

Five days later, however, Harold II decisively defeated his brother-in-law and brother at the battle of Stamford Bridge.

But he had little time to celebrate his victory, having to immediately march south from Yorkshire to encounter a mighty invasion force, led by Duke William of Normandy, that had landed at Hastings, in East Sussex.

Harold's battle-hardened but exhausted force of Anglo-Saxon soldiers confronted the Normans on October 14 in a battle subsequently depicted on the Bayeux tapestry – a 23ft. long strip of embroidered linen thought to have been commissioned eleven years after the event by the Norman Odo of Bayeux.

Harold drew up a strong defensive position at the top of Senlac Hill, building a shield wall to repel Duke William's cavalry and infantry.

The Normans suffered heavy losses, but through a combination of the deadly skill of their archers and the ferocious determination of their cavalry they eventually won the day.

Anglo-Saxon morale had collapsed on the battlefield as word spread through the ranks that Harold had been killed – the Bayeux Tapestry depicting this as having happened when the English king was struck by an arrow to the head.

Amidst the carnage of the battlefield, it was difficult to identify Harold – the last of the Anglo-Saxon kings.

Some sources assert William ordered his body to be thrown into the sea, while others state it was secretly buried at Waltham Abbey.

What is known with certainty, however, is

that William in celebration of his great victory founded Battle Abbey, near the site of the battle, ordering that the altar be sited on the spot where Harold was believed to have fallen.

William was declared King of England on December 25, and the complete subjugation of his Anglo-Saxon subjects followed.

Those Normans who had fought on his behalf were rewarded with the lands of Anglo-Saxons, many of whom sought exile abroad as mercenaries.

Within an astonishingly short space of time, Norman manners, customs and law were imposed on England – laying the basis for what subsequently became established 'English' custom and practice.

In 1282, by which time most of Wales had come under Anglo-Norman rule, final rebellion against this was crushed by England's Edward I, and it is from this date that the heir apparent to the British throne has borne the title of Prince of Wales.

An abortive rebellion was led in the early fifteenth century by the freedom fighter Owain Glyndŵr, while in the following century, under Henry VIII, Wales was 'incorporated' into the English kingdom; in 1707, in common with Scotland, Wales became part of the United Kingdom.

Flourishing not only in their original heartland of Wales but also throughout the British Isles, bearers of the Lloyd name feature prominently in the historical record.

Chapter three:

Risky business

From humble beginnings in a small London coffee shop to magnificent premises in the city's Lime Street, Lloyd's is the famous British corporate body that has been involved in the insurance market since the late seventeenth century.

More properly known as Lloyd's of London, its roots stretch back to Lloyd's Coffee House, opened by Edward Lloyd in about 1688 in Tower Street.

Lloyd, thought to have been born in about 1648, was responsible for making his coffee house a popular meeting place for merchants, ship owners and sailors who would gather there to obtain the reliable shipping news that he provided and to discuss insurance deals.

In late 1691, by which time the official Lloyd's of London insurance market and other related insurance and shipping businesses had been established, the coffee house relocated to new premises in Lombard Street and quickly became a hive of activity.

Edward Lloyd died in 1713, while in 1774 the business partners involved in the insurance scheme formed themselves into a committee and took over premises at the Royal Exchange as the Society of Lloyd's.

With the motto *Fidentia – Confidence –* Lloyd's now operates as a partially mutualised market place where a number of financial backers known as underwriters – also known as 'members', or 'names' – pool their financial resources to spread insurance risk.

Although still heavily involved in the provision of insurance in the world of international shipping, Lloyd's also provides insurance in a diverse range of other areas that include fine art, kidnap and ransom.

Some of the rather more unusual policies they have written include insuring Rolling Stones' guitarist Keith Richards' fingers, the legs of Marlene Dietrich, Tina Turner and Betty Grable, the food gourmet Egon Ronay's taste buds, the vocal cords of singers Whitney Houston, Celine Dion, Bruce Springsteen and Bob Dylan and the 'trademark' nose of the late American comedian Jimmy Durante.

Designed by the acclaimed British architect Richard Rogers and completed in 1986, the imposing premises of Lloyd's of London are now located at 1 Lime Street, London.

Continuing an early tradition, in what is known as its Underwriting Room there stands the famous Lutine Bell.

Originally, this was struck when a ship was overdue for arrival at its destination port. If the vessel was safe, the bell would be rung twice, while if it had sunk it was rung once.

The bell is now only used for ceremonial purposes such as Britain's annual Remembrance Day when it is rung once.

Meanwhile the original frontage of Edward Lloyd's Coffee House in Tower Street is still owned by Lloyd's of London and is on proud display at the National Maritime Museum, Greenwich.

In the frequently cut-throat world of politics, David Lloyd George was the great early twentieth century British Liberal Party politician and statesman born in 1863 in Chorlton-on-Medlock, Manchester and who, when only a few weeks old, moved back with his family to his parents' native Wales.

His father died when he was aged one and his mother, Elizabeth, moved with the family to her native Llanystumdwy, Caernarvonshire to live with her brother Richard Lloyd, a shoemaker.

It was because this uncle, Richard Lloyd, had

exercised such a profound and beneficial influence on his early life that Lloyd George, who had been born 'David George', later added 'Lloyd' to his surname in his honour.

With the encouragement and support of his uncle, Lloyd George studied and qualified as a lawyer in 1885 and set up a thriving legal practice in partnership with his brother William.

But his horizons were set far beyond legal practice and the valleys of his native Wales and it was through his keen interest in the politics of the day that in 1890 he was elected Liberal MP for Carnarvon Boroughs – making him at the time the youngest MP in the House of Commons.

His rise through the political ranks was meteoric.

As Prime Minister of the United Kingdom, he led the First World War coalition government, from 1916 to 1922, and served from 1926 to 1931 as Leader of the Liberal Party.

Representing Britain at the Versailles Peace Conference at the end of the First World War, he prophetically argued that punishing defeated Germany too harshly with crippling financial penalties could create massive unrest in the country and possibly lead to another war, while he is also recognised as having laid the foundations of Britain's Welfare State.

This was through pioneering legislation that includes the Education Act of 1918 that raised the school leaving age to 14, the Housing and Town Planning Act of 1919 that enabled local authorities, through the provision of special subsidies, to build much-needed homes, and the Unemployment Insurance Act of 1920 that extended National Insurance to an extra eleven million workers.

Raised to the Peerage of the United Kingdom in the same year of his death in 1945 as Earl Lloyd-George of Dwyfor and Viscount Gwynedd, he was named in 2002 as among the 100 Greatest Britons following a UK-wide vote, while a poll of academics voted him the third greatest British Prime Minister of the twentieth century.

Also in the world of British politics, John Selwyn Brooke Lloyd, better known as Selwyn Lloyd, was the leading Conservative party politician born in Cheshire in 1904.

Formerly a member of the Liberal Party, he later became a member of what was known as the 'Young Turks' faction of the Conservative Party, who argued for major policy changes.

A skilled House of Commons debater, he served as Foreign Secretary from 1955 to 1960 and from 1960 until 1962 as Chancellor of the Exchequer.

Elected Speaker of the House of Commons in 1971, he served in the post until his retirement from politics two years before his death in 1978 after being raised to the Peerage of the United Kingdom as Baron Selwyn-Lloyd of Wirral in the County of Merseyside.

From politics to the world of journalism, Terence Ellis Lloyd, better known as Terry Lloyd, was the British television journalist killed by U.S. troops in a 'friendly fire' incident in March of 2003 while covering the invasion of Iraq.

Born in 1952 in Derby, he worked for a time with the Raymonds News Agency before joining Independent Television News (ITN) in 1983.

Specialising in coverage of the Middle East, he broke the news in 1988 that Iraqi leader Saddam Hussein had used chemical weapons in Halabja, resulting in the horrific deaths of 5,000 Kurds.

The first journalist to enter war-torn Kosovo in the former Yugoslavia in 1999, it was while covering the invasion of Iraq that he and his team were caught in crossfire between U.S. and Iraqi troops near the Shatt Al Basra Bridge in Basra.

The journalist's body and that of his interpreter Hussein Osman were later recovered, while his French cameraman Frédéric Nérac is still officially classed as missing, presumed dead.

Only the Belgian cameraman Daniel Demoustier survived, while it was later determined that Lloyd and Osman had been shot by U.S. forces on the road to Basra.

In the creative world of architecture, Frank Lloyd Wright was the iconic American architect born Frank Lincoln Wright in 1867 in the farming community of Richland Center, Wisconsin.

Adding 'Lloyd' to his surname after his marriage to the schoolteacher Anna Lloyd Jones, he became famed as an exponent of 'organic architecture' – where structures are carefully designed to blend in with their environment.

Also a leader of what became known as the Prairie School of Architecture, he died in 1959 – the recipient of a number of honours that include Gold Medal Awards from the American Institute of Architects and the Royal Institute of British Architects.

Chapter four:

On the world stage

Born in London in 1870, Matilda Alice Victoria Wood was the popular late nineteenth and early twentieth century English music hall singer, actress and comedienne better known by her stage name of Marie Lloyd.

Known as the "Queen of Music Hall", she was aged only fifteen when she enjoyed success with her hit song *The Boy I Love is Up in the Gallery*, while she quickly became a star attraction on the stages of London's West End.

The daughter of a waiter and dressmaker and costume designer, she became known for a string of hit songs that include her 1914 wartime *Now You've Got your Khaki On*, *Oh Mr Porter What Shall I Do* and *My Old Man (Said Follow the Van)*.

Despite her fame and success, she had led a troubled life and died virtually penniless in 1922 after taking unwell during a performance at London's Alhambra Theatre – while as an indication of her popularity more than 50,000 people lined the route to her burial in Hampstead Cemetery.

First coming to prominence in the 1980s through his role of Jim Ignatowski in the television sitcom *Taxi*, **Christopher Lloyd** is the American actor born in 1938 in Stamford Connecticut.

Taking to the stage when aged 14, he has gone on to enjoy big screen credits that include the role of Uncle Fester in *The Addams Family* and its sequel *Addams Family Values* and as the eccentric inventor Emmett "Doc" Brown in the *Back to the Future* trilogy of science fiction films.

He is an uncle of the actor and musician **Sam Lloyd, Jr.**, best known for his roles in American television series that include *Scrubs*, *The West Wing*, *Malcolm in the Middle* and *Desperate Housewives*.

Born in 1963 in Vermont, he also sings with the Capella group The Blanks and plays bass guitar in the Beatles tribute band The Butties.

Recognised along with Charlie Chaplin and Buster Keaton as one of the most influential comedians and actors of the silent film era, **Harold Lloyd** was born in 1893 in Burchard, Nebraska of proud Welsh roots through his paternal grandparents.

He moved with his family to California when aged 19 and, after having acted since childhood in a number of vaudeville acts, formed a partnership with fellow actor and film director Hal Roach.

Roach had his own film studio, and this became a showcase for the talents of Lloyd and others.

Major screen credits include the 1923 *Safety Last!*, that hair-raisingly features a dare-devil Lloyd clinging from the outside of a skyscraper and is noted in the American Film Institute's List of 100 Most Thrilling Movies; the 1923 *Why Worry* and the 1924 *The Kid Brother* and *Speedy*.

The recipient of two stars on the Hollywood Walk of Fame and honoured in 1953 with a special Academy Award for being "a master comedian and a good citizen", he died in 1971.

Born in 1989 in Fort Collins, Colorado **Jake Lloyd** is the American actor best known for his role of the young Anakin Skywalker in the 1999 *Star Wars Episode 1: The Phantom Menace*, the first film in the Star Wars prequel trilogy.

Other film credits include the 1996 *Unhook the Stars*, the 1996 *Jingle All the Way* and, from 1998, *Hosts*.

Best known for his role of Ianto Jones in the popular British television *Doctor Who* spin-off series

Torchwood, **Gareth David Lloyd** is the Welsh actor born in 1980 in Bettws, Newport.

Other screen credits include *Casualty*, *The Bill*, the short film *A Very British Cover-Up* and the role of Rhys Hopkins in the television medical drama *Holby City*.

Also on British television screens, **Siân Lloyd** is best known as a presenter of *ITV Weather Forecast* – for which she won the Television and Radio Industries Club (TRIC) Award in 2005 and 2007 for Best TV Weather Presenter.

Born in 1958 in Maesteg, Bridgend, in Wales and the daughter of two teachers and the recipient of qualifications in meteorology, she was also romantically linked for a time to the former Liberal Democrat Member of Parliament (MP) Lembit Öpik.

Behind the camera lens, **Frank Lloyd** was the award-winning Scottish film director, screenwriter and producer born in Glasgow in 1886.

One of the founders of the Academy of Motion Pictures and Sciences and serving as its president from 1934 to 1935, he won his own Academy Award for his work on the 1929 *The Divine Lady*.

Also the recipient in 1935 of a Best Director

nomination for his work on *Mutiny on the Bounty*, he died in 1960.

Bearers of the Lloyd name have also excelled in the highly competitive world of sport.

On the tennis court, **John Lloyd**, born in 1954 in Leigh-on-Sea, Essex is the English former professional player who, in a distinguished career, reached one Grand Slam singles final and won three Grand Slam mixed doubles titles.

Formerly married to the American tennis player Chris Evert and a brother of the tennis player David Lloyd, he now pursues a successful career as a television commentator on the game.

On the fields of European football, **Laurence Lloyd**, born in 1948 in Bristol, is the English former central defender who, in addition to playing for clubs throughout the 1970s that include Liverpool and Nottingham Forest, also played for the England national team.

On the motor racing circuit, **Richard Lloyd** was the British driver and founder of sports and touring teams born in 1945.

The winner of a number of British Saloon Car Championships and the founder in 1978 of GTi Engineering – running Audi 80s and Volkswagen Golf

GTIs – he was killed in March of 2008, along with four others who included British Touring Car Championship driver David Leslie, when their private jet aircraft crashed after take-off from the outskirts of London en route to Paris.

In the rough and tumble that is the game of rugby, **Bobby Lloyd**, born in Crickhowell in 1888, was the Welsh international scrum-half who, in addition to playing club rugby for Pontypool and county rugby for Monmouthshire, earned seven caps playing for his nation from 1913 to 1914; he died in 1930.

Born in 1943 in Pontycmer, **John Lloyd** is the Welsh former international player who captained his national team in 1972 and who, in addition to playing club rugby for Bridgend and county rugby for Glamorgan, was a coach of the national team from 1980 to 1982.

On the darts board, **Colin Lloyd** is the English professional player, born in 1973 in Colchester, Essex and nicknamed "Jaws" who won the 2004 World Grand Prix and the 2005 World Matchplay.

On the cricket pitch, **Clive Lloyd** is the West Indies former cricketer who was named *Wisden* Cricketer of the Year in 1971.

Born in 1944 in Georgetown, Demerara,

Guyana, the left-handed batsman is the recipient of a CBE while in 2005 he was made an honorary officer of the Order of Australia for his services to the sport.

Bearers of the Lloyd name have also gained recognition in the world of music.

A contestant in the 2010 series of the British television music talent show *The X Factor*, **Cher Lloyd** is the singer, songwriter and model born in 1993 in Malvern, Worcestershire.

Despite coming fourth in the contest, she nevertheless was immediately signed to a recording contract and has since gone on to enjoy hits that include her 2011 single *Swagger Jagger* and albums that include *Sticks+Stones*.

On Australian shores, **Alex Lloyd**, born Alexander Wasilien in Sydney in 1974, is the best-selling singer and songwriter whose hit albums include his 1999 *Black the Sun*, the 2001 *Watching Angels Mend* and, from 2005, the eponymous *Alex Lloyd*.

One musically-talented family of the proud name of Lloyd – in the form of 'Lloyd Webber' – is one that includes the composer and impresario of musical theatre **Andrew Lloyd Webber** and his brother the renowned cellist **Julian Lloyd Webber**.

Born in London in 1948, the son of the organist and composer William Lloyd Webber and the violinist and pianist Jean Hermione Webber, Andrew Lloyd Webber is the recipient of an impressive fourteen Ivor Novello Awards, seven Grammy Awards, seven Tony Awards and seven Olivier Awards.

Known for works composed along with lyricist Tim Rice that include the 1965 *The Likes of Me*, the 1968 *Joseph and the Amazing Technicolor Dreamcoat*, the 1970 *Jesus Christ Superstar* and the 1976 *Evita* – in addition to works with other lyricists – he is also the recipient of a knighthood.

Born in 1951 and described as "the doyen of British cellists", his younger brother Julian Lloyd Webber is the musician whose works include his 1984 *Travels with my Cello*, the 2003 *Elegy*, the 2011 *The Art of Julian Lloyd Webber* and, from 2012, *Evening Songs*.